Sikhs, Jews and Hindus in Northern Ireland

Local People
Global Faiths

GW00725999

Colourpoint Educational

James Nelson
Norman Richardson

© James Nelson, Norman Richardson
and Colourpoint Books 2005

ISBN 1 904242 32 4

8 7 6 5 4 3 2 1

Layout and design: Colourpoint Books
Cover design: Malcolm Johnston
Printed by: Universities Press (Belfast) Ltd

Colourpoint Books
Colourpoint House
Jubilee Business Park
21 Jubilee Road
Newtownards
Co Down
BT23 4YH

Tel: 028 9182 0505
Fax: 028 9182 1900
E-mail: info@colourpoint.co.uk
Web-site: www.colourpoint.co.uk

Picture credits:

All pictures by the authors and student researchers except the
following:

Northern Ireland Inter-Faith Forum 2004 calendar 7 (also p. 4)
Supreet Vaid (Creative Art Graphics) 8 (right), 14 (also p. 4)
Clare Agnew 11
Strathclyde University 16 (bottom left), 20, 39 (left), 40, 51, 55
(top left)
World Religions Photo Library / Photographers Direct 19
Norman Johnston 27 (bottom), 31 (Synagogue interior &
exterior), 32, 34, 35 (bottom), 36 (also p. 4), 41, 43, 44,
49 (top)
Getty Images 27 (top), 48, 61
Children of the Belfast Jewish Community for the "We're Here
Too" exhibition © 2004 29 (bottom), 30, 31 (bottom right),
37 (right – also p. 4)
OFMDFM/Harrison Photography 35 (top)
Martin Louis 56
Nisha Tandon, Indian Community Centre Belfast 58 (left)
Sharada Bhat 59 (bottom)
Gary Skinner 62

Cover image courtesy of Photos.com

The extracts on pages 34 and 43 appear by kind permission of
Blackstaff Press and RE Today Services respectively.

All copyright has been acknowledged to the best of our ability.
We apologise for any inadvertent omissions, which we shall
endeavour to correct in any future edition.

James Nelson has been a
Head of RE and is now a
lecturer in Religious Studies at
Stranmillis University College,
Belfast. He has written several
RE textbooks for schools.

Norman Richardson teaches
Religious Studies at Stranmillis
University College, Belfast.
He has a long-standing
involvement in inter-church
and inter-faith issues and has
written and lectured regularly
in the field of religious and
cultural diversity.

The authors are grateful to a number of people without whom
this book would not have been possible:

• the Stranmillis University College students who put
considerable time and energy into meeting members of the
various faith communities to collect information, carry out
interviews, take photographs, and assist and advise in the
writing up of their material: **Victoria Walsh** (Sikhism),
Joanne Cardwell (Judaism) and **Jill Stringer** (Hinduism);

• the members of the faith communities, including the
young people featured throughout, who gave their time to
contribute to the accuracy and authenticity of this book:
    Mrs PK Sandhu, Mr GS Sandhu and other members of
        their families from Londonderry
    the Kular family from Londonderry
    Rabbi Avraham Citron
    Dr Katy Radford and her daughters – Jasmine and Grace
    the Angel family from Belfast
    the Taylor family (now in Manchester)
    Paula Tabakin (Community Development and Information
        Officer with the Belfast Jewish Community)
    Mrs Sharada Bhat (Belfast Indian Community Centre) and
        her family
    Mrs Nisha Tandon (Belfast Indian Community Centre)
    the Sridhar, Kashyap and Somasundram families from
        Belfast
    the Janarthanan family from Ballymena;

• all other parents who kindly gave permission for photographs
of their children to be used in this book; and

• the Northern Ireland Inter-Faith Forum
(interfaithni@stran.ac.uk) for its support and encouragement,
and for their assistance in providing contacts with the young
members of the various faith communities featured in this
book.

Contents

WebQuests for each religion are available at www.colourpoint.co.uk/extra/localglobal

Introduction

Faith communities in Northern Ireland

When it comes to religion, Northern Ireland is world famous, but often for all the wrong reasons – religious divisions, disagreements and fighting.

Everyone seems to be either Protestant or Catholic and it's important to be one or the other. It affects where you live, who your friends are, what sports you play, what school you go to, who you vote for, and even who you marry.

But is this really true? Is everyone either Protestant or Catholic? What about those people who aren't religious at all? What about those who are Sikh, Jewish, Hindu or of other faiths?

A rich mix

Northern Ireland isn't a Christian-only community any more. In recent years it has become a place where there is a rich mix of different **ethnic groups** and religious traditions. The largest ethnic group, of over 4,000 people, is the Chinese community.

Apart from Christianity the religious traditions with most members in Northern Ireland are **Islam**, **Hinduism**, **Sikhism**, the **Bahá'í Faith**, **Judaism** and **Buddhism**.

Muslim (Islam)	1,943
Hindu	825
Buddhist	533
Jewish	365
Bahá'í	254
Sikh	219
(NI census figures for 2001)	

Why study religion?

As you study different religions you will be finding out about the wider world but you will also be finding out more about the people who live around you in Northern Ireland.

Maybe there are people you didn't know about at all.

Maybe there are people you knew were there but you didn't know anything about.

Hopefully you'll also find out more about yourself. You'll be able to think about some of the important questions about life that all religions are concerned with.

You should also develop some valuable skills on the way.

Activities

A diversity survey

In groups, think of examples of people, businesses or organisations who are part of your town or community and who belong to religions other than Christianity or to different ethnic backgrounds.

Celebrating difference

As a class, think of different ways you might celebrate the variety of religions and cultures in your school or community. Think particularly of minority groups.

Discuss:

- how each tradition might be included in assemblies and RE classes

- how you might learn more about the religions, and their customs and culture

- ways in which you might celebrate important occasions or festivals

Draw up an action plan which shows the ideas you have, when they would happen, how they would be organised, and who would be involved.

A calendar of special days and festivals

A helpful way to start finding out about any religion is to find out about their festivals and celebrations.

You could begin by designing a calendar which would include festivals and special days of two religions that you will be studying.

To help you find out when the special days occur you might look at a calendar produced by the Northern Ireland Inter-Faith Forum. You can also find out about religious festivals online (www.bbc.co.uk/religion).

Once you've made your calendar you could plan to mark some of the special occasions in some way. For example, you could hold a special school assembly, design a poster, or invite a visitor to come to your class.

Timeline 3000 BCE – 2100 CE
(not to scale)

HINDUISM
(Began circa 3000 BCE;
Vedas written *c.* 800 BCE)

JUDAISM
(Abraham b. *c.* 2166 BCE;
Moses led Jews out of Israel
*c.*1300 BCE)

BUDDHISM
(Siddharta Gotama b. *c.*
580 BCE)

CHRISTIANITY
(Jesus b. *c.* 5 BCE)

ISLAM
(Muhammad b. 570 CE)

SIKHISM
(Guru Nanak b. 1469 CE)

BAHÁ'Í
(Bahá'u'lláh b. 1817 CE)

Word Bank

Before Common Era (BCE)/Common Era (CE):
The terms BCE and CE are alternatives to
the Christian dating system BC and AD.
They can be used by all religions. They do
not change the year numbers in any way.

Circa: a Latin word which means 'about' or
'around'. It is often placed beside dates
to show they are approximate, and is
abbreviated as *c.*

Diversity: variety and difference

Ethnic group: the race or nationality you
belong to

Sikhism

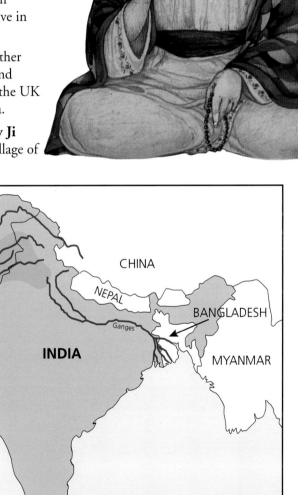

*Guru Nanak –
founder of Sikhism*

What is Sikhism?

The Sikh religion began in the state of **Punjab** in India in the second half of the fifteenth century (1400s). It is one of the youngest of the world religions. There are around 20 million Sikhs in the world today. About 80 per cent of them live in North-West India and Pakistan.

There are communities of Sikhs in many other countries, including parts of Africa, Europe and North America. About 500,000 Sikhs live in the UK which has the largest number outside of India.

Sikhism was founded by **Guru Nanak Dev Ji** (1469–1539), who was born in the Punjab village of Talvandi, which is now in Pakistan.

AFGHANISTAN

IRAN

PAKISTAN

Indus

CHINA

NEPAL

Ganges

BANGLADESH

INDIA

MYANMAR

Punjab

In 1947 the Punjab was divided between Pakistan and India. At this time the majority of Sikhs moved to the Indian side of the border.

Guru Nanak travelled widely and preached a simple message that all people were equal in front of God, no matter who they were. His followers became known as Sikhs (which means 'pupils' or 'disciples').

There were nine more **Gurus** after him who developed the Sikh message. Their writings and the writings of 31 other writers of different faiths and backgrounds were compiled into a holy book, the **Adi Granth**.

Just before he died in 1708, the tenth Guru, **Guru Gobind Singh**, declared that he was the last of the human Gurus and that the position would be passed on to these Sikh scriptures.

Since then the scriptures have become known as the **Guru Granth Sahib**.

A picture of Guru Gobind Singh

The ten Gurus and dates of their leadership

Guru Nanak (b. 1469–1539)

Guru Angad (1539–52)

Guru Amar (1552–74)

Guru Ram (1574–81)

Guru Arjan (1581–1606)

Guru Har Gobind (1606–44)

Guru Har Rai (1644–61)

Guru Har Krishan (1661–64)

Guru Tegh Bahadur (1664–75)

Guru Gobind Singh (1675–1708)

Sikh worship

A Sikh place of worship is called a **gurdwara**. The central feature is the Guru Granth Sahib. A gurdwara normally also has a community kitchen (**langar**) attached. Any visitor of any faith is welcome to join in a meal there.

A special place for Sikhs is the **Golden Temple of Amritsar** (also known as Harimandir Sahib, meaning 'God's temple') in the Punjab.

Sikhs believe that God's presence is everywhere, so there are no places which are more holy than any other, but many Sikhs like to visit the Golden Temple because of its connection with their history and the Gurus.

The Golden Temple

The **Khanda** is the symbol of Sikhism and is made up of three parts.

The upright double edged-sword in the centre represents truth and divine knowledge.

The circle around the sword represents the perfection of God and that he is without beginning or end.

The two curved swords around the outside represent spiritual and worldly authority and remind Sikhs that they must give equal attention to their spiritual lives and others in society.

What Sikhs believe

Sikhs have an individual relationship with the one God, with whom they aim to achieve unity.

They do not use statues or images of God.

They believe that by living a truthful life they can reach God and that salvation can be found through God's grace.

A truthful life consists of remembering God at all times, earning your own livelihood, and sharing your time and wealth with the community.

Sikhism in Northern Ireland

The earliest Sikh immigrants to Northern Ireland were mostly soldiers who had been in the British army. Others arrived in the late 1920s. Most settled in or near the city of Derry.

The present Sikh community still lives mainly in the north-west of Northern Ireland. There are about 20 families in all – about 200 people.

Activity

WebQuest

Explore this religion further by trying the WebQuest at www.colourpoint.co.uk/extra/localglobal

Word Bank

Gurdwara: means 'door of the Guru' – the Sikh place of worship where the Guru Granth Sahib is kept

Guru: a religious teacher

Guru Granth Sahib: originally known as the Adi Granth – Sikh scriptures containing writings of the Gurus as well as works by Hindu and Muslim writers

Khanda: symbol of Sikhism

Langar: the free kitchen found in a gurdwara, serving only vegetarian meals; also the name for the communal meal served there

Who am I?

Meet two of the young people who are part of the Sikh community in Londonderry – Mani and Rena Kular. There are seven members of the Kular family – Granny, Mum, Dad and four children: two boys (Mani and Harjesh) and two girls (Rena and Yasmin).

Read Rena and Mani's profiles, then complete the activity.

Profile

Name: *Mani Kular*

Age: *11*

School: *Foyle and Londonderry College*

Favourite subject: *PE*

Special interests: *rugby and football*

Favourite music: *rap music*

Favourite food: *chick sticks, cheese pancakes, mashed potatoes and beans*

The best thing about being a Sikh: *going to India*

Profile

Name: *Rena Kular*

Age: *13*

School: *Foyle and Londonderry College*

Favourite subject: *Maths*

Special interests: *music and hockey*

Favourite music: *R&B and pop*

Favourite food: *Indian – chicken tikka, makhan sauce and naan bread*
Other – McDonald's McChicken Premier Meal and milkshake

The best thing about being a Sikh: *going to our temple – the gurdwara, learning another language (Punjabi), and talking about Sikhism to my friends who like to know all about it*

Activity

Identity collage

1. Design an identity collage for Mani and Rena by writing both their names in the middle of a page and illustrating the blank space around this with pictures and symbols which say something about them. Look at the picture on the opposite page ('Champagne Brothers' by Clare Agnew) for an example of how a local artist has created an identity collage.

2. Now design your own collage which says something about you. It should show your hobbies, sports you practice, and other things you like. You should also try to include something about your beliefs and opinions, and what matters most to you. Once you've completed your drawing look at the work of others in your class.

What conclusions can you draw? In comparing the pictures what does it say about the range of identities of people in your class?

Dress

Most days of the week Sikh young people in Northern Ireland do not dress very differently from others their age.

Adults in the Sikh community are more recognisable. Some of the men wear turbans and women wear the **salwar** (trousers) and **kameeze** (tunic top). Some women also wear a **Kara** bangle to remind them that God is perfect and has no beginning or end.

At the gurdwara there is a dress code, so when Sikhs go to worship there they do dress slightly differently.

Everyone must have his or her head covered during worship. Boys wear a scarf called a **patka** and girls and women wear a shawl called a **dupatta**. Men must cover their heads too so those who do not wear a turban must wear a patka.

At home

Sikh homes usually contain several important religious objects such as pictures of the Sikh Gurus (particularly Guru Nanak), a picture or flag with the Sikh Khanda symbol on it, the **Ik Onkar** symbol, a prayer book, and a picture of the Golden Temple of Amritsar.

Ik Onkar means 'There is only one God'.

A week in the life of a Sikh teenager

Yasmin: *"On a Monday and Wednesday our family sits down to eat a traditional Indian meal consisting of a meat dish such as chicken or pork, but no beef as we believe the cow is sacred. We also eat a vegetable dish along with home-made yoghurt and some Indian breads."*

Rena: *"On Saturday I go to our temple for a Punjabi class from 1–2 pm where I learn how to read, write and speak my Indian language."*

Yasmin: *"Sunday is the day when I attend our temple for worship. I get up about 10.30 and have a shower as washing before praying is important in our religion. I then go to the temple where I sit for about one and a half hours listening to the **granthi** sing and pray. I then go to langar, which is when we eat food together. After this I go out with a few friends or spend time with my family."*

Word Bank

Dupatta: shawl used by women to cover their head during worship

Granthi: sometimes called a priest but in reality can be any man or woman who can read the Guru Granth Sahib. Each gurdwara usually has a person who has been specially trained to read from this.

Ik Onkar: means 'There is only one God' – the opening words of the **Mool Mantar**, a Sikh statement of faith (see page 17)

Kara: a steel bracelet which symbolises the eternal nature of God

Patka: boy's headscarf

Salwar-kameeze: trousers and tunic top worn by Sikh women

Who are we?

The Northern Ireland Sikh Association was formed in 1990 and shortly afterwards the Northern Ireland Sikh Cultural and Community Centre was set up in the Waterside district of Derry.

The Sikh community

The idea of community is very important to Sikhs. The word they use to refer to it is **panth**. Sikh panth can be all those people in the world who call themselves Sikhs, or it can refer to a local group of believers. At a local level the Sikh gurdwara is a symbol of the Sikh community.

One very important part of community life in Sikhism is that all members are equal. Guru Amar Das said:

"All are created from the seed of God. There is the same clay in the whole world, the potter (God) makes many kinds of pots."

This means that men and women have equal roles in Sikhism. There are no priests or religious leaders with special powers or duties. Everyone is regarded as the same in the eyes of God.

Family life is also a central part of the Sikh tradition. Many Sikhs in Londonderry live in an extended family with different generations and different branches of the family sharing the same house.

This means that the home is a place for learning and sharing the faith.

Langar

Langar, or 'Guru's Kitchen', is a communal meal which is part of community life in the gurdwara. It is offered free to anyone who wishes to attend. Sikhs believe it is a religious duty to care for others and this is an example of how they do so in a very practical way.

In the gurdwara in Derry different women from the community prepare the food each week. The young people are also involved in preparing food and tidying up after the meal.

While Sikhs are free to eat meat, the food served at the langar is vegetarian so that no-one is left out. The food is served on trays and usually consists of lentil soup, vegetables, rice and chapatis. Indian tea is usually served after the meal.

Yasmin Kular, Mani and Rena's sister, is doing her A levels and her favourite subject is Home Economics. Here's what she thinks about being part of the Sikh community:

"One of the most important things about belonging to the Sikh community is having so many festivals and having a great time with my friends and family who are of a similar background to myself. I enjoy going to the gurdwara to listen to the hymns as it's the only time in the week I can hear religious songs that are in Punjabi. At times, though, it's a challenge belonging to the Sikh community – sometimes the older generation can be quite strict and they think you shouldn't cut your hair or go out too often with your friends."

A typical langar meal

The Derry Gurdwara

Serving food at the langar

Sikhs in India preparing food for the langar

Activity

On community

Draw a spider diagram, with your name at the centre. Show all the groups you belong to. These might include sports clubs, teams, music groups, youth clubs, your class in school, family networks and religious organisations.

Think about some good things and some bad things about being involved in these different groups. For example:

- What responsibilities are involved in belonging?
- Are there many demands made on you in the different groups?
- What makes belonging to a group or a community worthwhile?

Now ask yourself how you might be a better group or community member.

Are there any groups you might consider joining which make a positive contribution to other people?

Activity

On equality

Choose one of the groups you belong to. Now think about how the group might be different if, as in Sikhism, everyone in the group was considered completely equal.

Complete a grid showing how it is now and how it would be different in areas such as:

- male and female roles
- leadership roles
- opportunities for young and old
- privileges and rewards
- authority and power.

Do you think your organisation would be better if it were more equal?

What practical measures might you take to improve its equality?

Are there times when treating everyone equally is not possible or practical? If so, how would you decide what roles or positions people should have?

Word Bank

Sikh panth: the Sikh community

How do we worship?

Sikhs do not have a set day for worship, although the community in Londonderry meet on a Sunday as this is the day when most people do not work and are free to attend. The service of worship is called **diwan**.

Inside the gurdwara

At the front of the main prayer hall is a raised platform (**manji**) and canopy (**chanani**) where the Guru Granth Sahib is set during worship.

A chauri

Before entering the prayer hall worshippers remove their shoes. Once inside, they walk towards the manji. They kneel and bow their heads to the floor, then place an offering – usually of money – in a bowl which is at the foot of the manji.

The manji and chanani

The bed where the Guru Granth Sahib is placed when it is not being read

The Guru Granth Sahib is regarded as the Word of God and is always treated with great respect. When it is being read during a service, a **chauri** – a special fan made of yak hair – is waved over it, and when it is not being used it 'sleeps' in a special raised bed at the rear of the prayer hall.

15

The worshippers then sit on the floor. Men sit on the left-hand side and women on the right. Children sit near the back of the hall as they usually leave during the service to have a Sunday school. They learn about their Sikh religion, culture and language.

A Sunday service of worship can last up to two hours. The majority of the service involves reading and singing from the Guru Granth Sahib. The worship is led by a granthi – a person responsible for reading the Guru Granth Sahib, who can be any respected member of the community.

© Religious Education

A granthi reading from the Guru Granth Sahib

Everyone is present for the climax of the service which is the sharing of **karah parshad**. This is a sweet food made from semolina, butter and sugar.

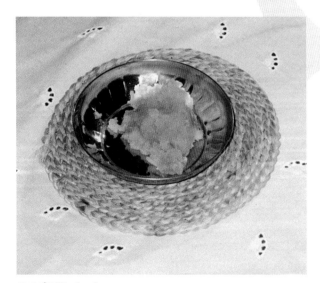

Karah parshad

The karah parshad can be blessed and distributed to worshippers by any Sikh adult and the children usually help by distributing tissues or kitchen roll.

A Sikh girl helps during the sharing of karah parshad

Activity

Showing respect

Sikhs show respect in different ways during a worship service.

Can you identify some of these ways?

As a class think about why people show respect to religious objects, people and places.

Do you think it is important to show respect to special objects, people or places of a religion if you do not belong to it?

Why?

Personal worship

Many Sikhs believe that worship is not only something done at the gurdwara, but is a way of life – devotion to God in everything. Many set aside time in the morning and evening to recite prayers and use meditation to focus their minds on God.

The Sikh concept of God

Sikhs believe there is only one God – **Waheguru**. The first page of the Guru Granth Sahib contains a statement of faith called the **Mool Mantar** which is a summary of the Sikh belief in God. You can read it in the panel below.

Sikhs think that God is beyond human understanding or description. They believe all religions are different ways that people have tried to get close to God.

No religion is wrong. Each is a different path to God. Each person must follow their own religion as best they can.

The opening words of the Mool Mantar are "Ik Onkar", which means "There is only one God". The symbol for Ik Onkar is an important and well-known symbol which Sikhs often display in their homes or in the gurdwara.

Mool Mantar

Ik Onkar: There is only one God

Sat Nam: Eternal Truth is his name

Karta Purakh: He is the creator

Nir Bhan: He is without fear

Nir Vair: He is without hate

Akal Murat: He is timeless and without form

Ajuni: Beyond birth and death

Saibhang: The enlightened one

Gur Parshad: He can be reached through the mercy and grace of the true Guru

Activity

Beliefs in God

The two quotations about God below are from a Sikh prayer.

"Just as seconds, minutes, hours, quarters of a day, lunar days, week days, months, are created by one sun and so are created many seasons by it, similarly God, who is One has many manifestations, so says Nanak ... "

Kirtan Sohila

"Your eyes are thousands, yet You have no eye; Your forms are thousands, yet You have no form. Your pure feet are thousands, yet You have no feet; You are without nose, yet You have a thousand noses; Your plays have, in this way, bewitched me. The same Light pervades all. This Light causes the light to shine within all. Through the Guru's advice the divine Light becomes visible. That, which pleases Him, constitutes His real worship."

Kirtan Sohila

In pairs, read one quotation each and try to explain to each other what it says about Sikh beliefs about God. Write these in a column on the left of a blank page.

Now add one other column which describes your own ideas about God.

If you don't believe in God you can write down what you think are the most important values to live by.

You could express your ideas in a picture or poem and share this with others in your class.

Word Bank

Chanani: a canopy above the manji

Chauri: a fan made of yak hairs which is waved over the Guru Granth Sahib

Diwan: service of congregational worship

Karah parshad: blessed food distributed during a Sikh service of worship

Manji: a raised platform where the Guru Granth Sahib is placed during worship

Mool Mantar: a Sikh statement of faith within the Guru Granth Sahib

Waheguru: 'Wonderful Lord', a Sikh name for God

What is there to celebrate?

Sikhs believe that every day is special, so a festival day is no more important than any other day, but they are still occasions of joy and celebration.

The two main festivals celebrated by Sikhs in Northern Ireland are **Baisakhi** (or Vaisakhi) and **Diwali** (or Divali).

Baisakhi

Baisakhi Day is usually on 13 or 14 April and is two celebrations rolled into one.

It is the Sikh New Year and also celebrates the founding of the Sikh **Khalsa** in 1699. Today Sikhs who make a special commitment to their faith still become members of the Khalsa. You can read more about the Khalsa and the history of Baisakhi on page 21.

In India, at Baisakhi celebrations there is usually a colourful street procession. The Guru Granth Sahib is carried around on a special platform and led by five Sikh men who represent the first five members of the Khalsa – the **Panj Piare** (see page 21).

The Sikh community in Northern Ireland celebrates Baisakhi with special services. For them it as a time to renew their own commitment to the faith.

"My favourite festival is Baisakhi. In India there are huge parades on the streets, special events in the gurdwara and the whole family gets together."
Hemdeep Aveleen Singh

Diwali

Diwali is a traditional festival in India to celebrate the end of the rainy season. It is celebrated by both Sikhs and Hindus.

Each religion has its own special story associated with the occasion. For both, symbols of light, such as candles, fireworks and festive lights, are an important part of Diwali celebrations. It is a very popular festival, particularly with young people:

"Diwali is one of my favourite festivals as it celebrates light and we have big parties and fireworks!"
Rena Kular

Why Sikhs celebrate Diwali

At Diwali time, Sikhs remember when the sixth Guru, Har Gobind, was to be released from prison just before the Diwali festival in 1619.

He refused to leave unless 52 Hindu rajas could be freed with him. The Emperor Jehangir said that he could take as many with him as could hold on to his cloak as he walked through a narrow gate.

Har Gobind had long tassels added to his cloak and when he walked through the gate all the rajas managed to hold on and were freed.

After being released, the Guru went to the Golden Temple at Amritsar where Sikhs had decorated the gurdwara and surrounding pool with lamps. The tradition of decorating the Golden Temple at Diwali continues today.

Activity

Celebrations

Diwali is often called a festival of light.

Can you imagine why light is such an important symbol in religious festivals?

Try to find out about festivals in other religions which have light as a central symbol.

Word Bank

Khalsa: a Sikh who has demonstrated his/her devotion to God and the Sikh faith through an **Amrit Ceremony**

Panj Piare: the five beloved ones – Sikhs who, according to tradition, demonstrated particular loyalty to their faith

World Religions Photo Library / Photographers Direct

Celebrating Diwali at a gurdwara in England

What gives life meaning?

Beliefs about life and death

Sikhs believe in **rebirth** or **reincarnation**. This is the idea that after death a person is reborn as a human or an animal. What you do, and the consequences of what you do (**karma**) in this life decide the position you achieve in the next life.

The goal of human life is to escape the cycle of birth, death and rebirth, and become one with God. This is called **mukti**.

In order to achieve mukti a Sikh must follow the teachings of the Gurus, meditate on the Name of God and perform **sewa** (service to others). They must also try to avoid five temptations (or **'the five thieves'**): **pride**, **lust**, **anger**, **greed**, and **worldly attachment**.

"Our service in the world gets us a seat in the Court of the Lord ... "

Guru Nanak

The Guru Granth Sahib

The Guru Granth Sahib means 'the teachings of the Gurus'. Sikhs believe that it is the Word of God. It is written in the Punjabi language and contains 3,384 hymns.

It was written over a period of 200 years and contains the writings of the Sikh Gurus, as well as writings from the Hindu and Muslim traditions.

"The Guru Granth Sahib is important to me personally. In particular I believe in the phrases 'There is only one God', and 'Men and women are equal'. I'm proud that they come from the Guru Granth Sahib."

Yasmin Kular

Commitment in Sikhism (The Five Ks)

In Sikhism there is a form of initiation for those who wish to make a special commitment to their faith and become a member of the Khalsa.

Khalsa means 'pure' and refers to Sikhs (men and women) who have devoted themselves to God through an **Amrit Ceremony**. They commit themselves to observance of the **Five Ks** and the **Sikh Code of Conduct**.

The Amrit Ceremony is carried out in private by five men who are already part of the Khalsa. They explain the meaning of the Code and sprinkle **amrit** (or 'nectar', made of sugar and water) five times into the eyes and five times onto the hair of the person being initiated.

Each time the amrit is sprinkled, the following words are said:

"Waheguru ji ka khalsa, Waheguru ji ki Fateh!"

This means: "The Khalsa is dedicated to God; victory ever is of Almighty Lord!"

© Religious Education
University of Strathclyde

The Five Ks

The Five Ks (Panj Kakke) are the 'uniform' of the Khalsa – symbols of Sikhism which outwardly show deeply-held beliefs.

Kesh: uncut hair. Sikh Khalsas must not cut any hair from their body. This shows their desire to live in harmony with the will of God. Men usually tie their hair up in a knot and cover it with a turban to keep it clean and protected.

Kangha: a comb. This is used to keep the hair neat and to demonstrate the need for spiritual discipline and control.

Kirpan: sword. This is usually a miniature sword which is worn on a belt or around the neck, depending on what size it is. It is a symbol of bravery and courage in defending what is right.

Kara: a bracelet made of steel. This symbolises the eternal (no beginning or end) nature of God, and the unity of Sikhs with God and with each other.

Kachera: long shorts. This is an undergarment worn by men and women as a practical and hygienic alternative to the traditional Indian dress of the time. They symbolise self-control and being ready to defend what is right.

Word Bank

Amrit Ceremony: a private ceremony in which Sikhs can dedicate themselves to God and become members of the Khalsa

Five Ks (Panj Kakke): objects which symbolise commitment to Sikhism

Mukti: means 'release' or 'liberation' and refers to liberation from rebirth

Reincarnation: the belief that after death a person is reborn as a human or an animal

Sewa: selfless service to others

Sikh Code of Conduct: a code containing important principles Sikhs try to live by

The beginning of the Khalsa

According to tradition, on Baisakhi Day in 1699 CE, Guru Gobind Singh asked a crowd if there was anyone prepared to give his life for the Guru.

Eventually one man stepped forward. Both men went into a tent and before long the Guru emerged from the tent with a blood-stained sword and asked for another volunteer.

Four more men came forward and each time the same thing happened.

However, when it seemed that all five men had been killed, the Guru came out of the tent and all the men came with him, still alive.

They had proved they were truly devoted Sikhs so the Guru sprinkled amrit on their hair and faces and they did the same to him.

He said that they were now the Panj Piare (five beloved ones).

This was the beginning of the Khalsa.

Activity

Commitment

Imagine you are a Sikh and you are thinking about becoming a member of the Khalsa.

In groups, talk about what kinds of reasons you might have for wanting or not wanting to join.

To make a commitment which is both inward and outward takes real devotion and bravery.

What other ways do people show commitment to religion?

Do you think that what you believe should make a difference to how you act and even what you wear?

Are there special occasions in your life when you have celebrated a decision or commitment?

What did you do to demonstrate your commitment to others?

How do I know what's right and wrong?

Sikhs are guided in how to live their lives by the words of the Guru Granth Sahib and the Sikh Code of Conduct. Underlying these teachings are some important principles, including:

- honest work
- sharing your time, abilities and money with others who are not as fortunate as you are
- sewa, which is service to others.

In all of these, Sikhs believe that equality and keeping God at the centre of life is all-important:

"As fragrance lives in a flower, and your reflection is in the mirror, so God lives in everything."

Guru Granth Sahib

Sewa

Sewa – selfless service – is at the heart of the Sikh faith.

The best known example of sewa is the langar meal which Sikhs provide for their community and anyone who wants to eat with them. Sikhs believe that they should offer service to everyone, no matter who they are.

"Sewa is helping out and doing work for free. Sometimes at the gurdwara, for example, I help to prepare and cook food or sometimes I clean the dishes."

Yasmin Kular

As well as the langar there are many other ways in which Sikhs can carry out sewa. These are often summarised as **Tan**, **Man** and **Dhan**:

- Tan is giving physical service such as cleaning or cooking.
- Man is mental service such as teaching others from the Guru Granth Sahib.
- Dhan is material service such as giving money to charity or giving your time to visit or care for someone.

Sikhs believe that performing sewa is like an act of worship because God is in all people. Therefore serving others is the same as serving God.

Activity

Serving others

Look at the different forms of service on the left. Think of as many examples of each as you can which Sikhs might do.

Do you think it is important to help other people?

Think of some ways in which you could be of service to others.

Serving food at langar

Summary of the Sikh Code of Conduct

Instructions

- There is only one God; worship and pray to Him alone.
- Always work hard, and share with others.
- Be truthful.
- Remember, women and men are equal.
- The whole human race is one. Distinctions of **caste**, colour, religion or class are wrong.
- Magic, omens, fasts, idols, and other ritual objects are unnecessary.
- Dress yourself in a simple and modest way.
- Sikh women should not wear the veil; neither should men or women make holes in their ears and noses. *[continued]*

- Live a married life; **celibacy** and **asceticism** are unnecessary.
- Put your faith in the Guru Granth Sahib.

Injunctions (given at the time of initiation)

- Do not cut your hair.
- Do not use tobacco.
- Do not eat **'ritual meat'**.
- Do not commit adultery.

Guru Nanak and the rich man

During his travels, Guru Nanak and a companion came one day to a town where they met a rich merchant, Bhai Bhago, who invited them to eat with him. He prepared expensive and elaborate food for the Guru and his companion, but Guru Nanak refused to eat it.

Instead he left and went to a poor farmer, Bhai Lalo, who was happy to share his small plate of food. When Bhai Bhago caught up with the Guru he asked him why he chose to eat stale scraps of food instead of from his banquet. Guru Nanak asked Bhai Bhago to go and get some of his food and bring it to him, which he did.

When he returned, the Guru took some of Bhai Bhago's food in one hand and some of Bhai Lalo's in the other and squeezed them both. From Bhai Lalo's food came milk but from Bhai Bhago's came blood.

The Guru said to Bhai Bhago, "Milk comes from Bhai Lalo's food because it is pure, but blood comes from yours because you have earned your money by cheating and dishonesty and through the hard work of others."

Bhai Bhago was ashamed and promised to work honestly, to be kind to his workers, and to share his riches with others.

What is the message Guru Nanak is trying to teach through this incident?

What might Sikhs today learn from this story?

How might they try to put what they have learnt into practice?

Activity

My code of conduct

Look at the Sikh Code of Conduct. Which rules do you agree with?

Try to design a code of conduct for yourself which summarises how you try to live.

Compare your code with others in your class. Are there any things in common?

Try to agree a code of conduct for your class, put it on a poster and display it in your classroom.

Guru Nanak

Word Bank

Asceticism: self-denial – rejecting worldly pleasures and comforts, often for religious reasons

Caste: the social class a person is seen to belong to

Celibacy: being unmarried, sometimes because of a religious vow

Ritual meat: a product of the ritual slaughter of animals, which is practised by members of some religions

Learning about and learning from Sikhism

As a result of working on this unit on Sikhism you should know about:

- Sikhism as a world religion
- the Sikh community in Northern Ireland
- how some Sikhs worship
- important Sikh festivals
- key Sikh beliefs
- some Sikh teaching about right and wrong

You should also have had an opportunity to reflect on the following themes from your own point of view:

- community
- identity
- equality
- respect
- commitment
- celebrations
- rules
- helping others

And you should have developed skills in:

- discussion
- thinking
- ICT
- working with others
- making presentations

Activity

Post-it

Complete the following three statements and write them on separate post-it notes.

After studying this chapter:

I have learned about Sikhism…

I have thought about issues of…

I have developed skills in…

Now stick your responses onto a large sheet of paper.

Have a class discussion and talk about some of the most important things that you have all learned from this unit.

You could write them down as headings and pin them up them in your classroom.

Activity

Evaluation

Now try to complete these statements honestly:

One thing I did very well during this unit was…

The reason I did well was…

One thing I could have done better was…

The reason I didn't do so well was…

Ways in which I want to improve my work in the future are…

Judaism

What is Judaism?

Judaism has a long history going back about 4,000 years.

It was the religion of the Hebrew tribes living in **Palestine** but wars over many centuries have scattered the Jews all over the world. This scattering of the Jews is called the **Diaspora**.

Since the early twentieth century (1900s) many Jews have moved back to Palestine, particularly since the end of World War II. There are about 18 million Jews throughout the world now. They are mainly in North America and Israel.

The modern state of **Israel** was set up in 1948. It is in the same area as Palestine. For many Jews, Israel is at the centre of their religion. They travel there to visit the **Western Wall** in Jerusalem. This is an important symbol of their faith and you can read about it in the panel at the top of the next page.

The traditional language of Judaism is **Hebrew** and a modern form of this language is still spoken by Israelis today.

King Solomon was a Jewish king who ruled in the tenth century BCE.

He built a Temple in Jerusalem which was the centre of worship and sacrifice.

The Temple was destroyed and rebuilt several times. The Romans destroyed it in 70 CE and it was never rebuilt after that.

The only part remaining is its Western Wall.

The Western Wall today

Varieties of Judaism

The main forms of Judaism are **Orthodox**, **Reform**, **Liberal**, **Conservative** and **Progressive**. Each has its own tradition.

What Jews believe

Jews believe in one God – the creator and absolute ruler of the universe who has a special relationship or **covenant** with the Jewish people based upon the promise made to **Abraham**:

"I will be your God and the God of your descendants."

Genesis 17:7

Abraham is a very important person in Jewish history – the Father of the Nation. He may have lived sometime around 1500–1200 BCE. He belonged to a **nomadic** tribe and Jews believe that he began the worship of the one true God.

Jews believe that God has given them laws to follow. The most important laws are the **Ten Commandments**, which are found in the **Torah** – the first five books of the Hebrew Bible. They were revealed to **Moses** by God. You will learn more about the Ten Commandments later.

In order to help them to understand the Torah many Jewish people also consult the **Talmud**. It is a large collection of ancient writings from the first few centuries CE.

God

The personal name of God (YHWH, usually written as **Yahweh**) is very holy and therefore never used by Jews. The Hebrew words **'Adonai'** (my Lord) or **'Ha-Shem'** (the Name) are spoken instead.

Jewish practices

Jews come together to worship on Saturdays at a **synagogue (shul)**. A synagogue is governed by its congregation and services are normally led by a **rabbi**.

In Orthodox Judaism, most of the synagogue service is conducted in the ancient language of Hebrew.

Jews in Northern Ireland

Jews have been in Ireland longer than any other small religious community. Some came in the seventeenth century (1600s).

The first synagogue was set up in Great Victoria Street, Belfast, in the 1840s when German Jews began to settle there because of their work in the linen trade. In the late nineteenth century (1800s) many Jews came to Belfast to escape **persecution** in Russia. A new synagogue had to be built for the growing community.

Throughout the years, there have been Jewish communities in Derry, Downpatrick and Lurgan. Since the mid-twentieth century, however, numbers have fallen, partly due to **emigration** to Israel. Probably the Troubles also made some Jews decide to leave.

David Rubinger / Getty Images

Chaim Herzog

Chaim Herzog is a 'famous son' of the Northern Ireland Jewish community. He was born in Belfast in 1918. His father was a rabbi.

In 1935 the family moved to Palestine where he worked as a lawyer and as a diplomat. When the new State of Israel was set up in 1948, he was elected as a politician.

In 1983 he became President of Israel and served for ten years. He died in 1997.

THIS PLAQUE COMMEMORATES THE LIFE OF
CHAIM HERTZOG
1918–1997
BORN BELFAST SEPTEMBER 17th 1918
PRESIDENT OF THE STATE OF ISRAEL 1983–1993
SON OF RABBI ISAAC HERTZOG
CHIEF RABBI OF THE STATE OF ISRAEL 1936–1958

Memorial plaque in the Belfast Synagogue

"Life for a religious Jew can be difficult in Northern Ireland. The community has shrunk to a tenth of its former size, but the Belfast Jewish community has added to Northern Ireland the colourful mosaic of Jewish culture, tradition and heritage."

Rabbi Citron

Word Bank

Covenant: the special agreement and relationship between God and the Jewish people

Diaspora: the scattering of Jews around the world

Emigration: leaving your own country to go to live in another one

Nomadic: moving around, not living in one place all the time

Persecution: being badly treated because of your race or beliefs

Rabbi: literally 'teacher' – an ordained Jewish member of the clergy

Shul: a **Yiddish** term used by Jews for the synagogue

Synagogue: Jewish place of worship

Talmud: a collection of writings by the early Jewish rabbis, including commentaries on the Torah and other scriptures

Ten Commandments: basic rules for conduct which, according to the Torah, were given to Moses on Mount Sinai

Torah: also known as **'the Law'** – can refer to either the first five books of the Bible, or the complete body of Jewish teaching

Western Wall: a surviving wall of the Jerusalem Temple, sometimes called the Wailing Wall, and a very symbolic place for Jews

Yiddish: a European Jewish language based on Hebrew and German

Activity

WebQuest

Explore this religion further by trying the WebQuest at www.colourpoint.co.uk/extra/localglobal

Who am I?

Adam Taylor and Zoe Angel are two young people who are members of the Jewish community in Northern Ireland.

Profile

Name: *Adam Taylor*

Age: *12*

School: *Rockport*

Favourite subjects: *Geography and Science*

Special interests: *swimming, rugby, violin, table tennis, chess and orchestra*

Favourite food: *pizza, chopped liver, and roast beef dinner*

Favourite Jewish festival: ***Chanukah*** and ***Yom Kippur***

My views on Judaism: *"I really enjoy celebrating the **Sabbath** with a special family meal on Friday nights."*

Profile

Name: *Zoe Angel*

Age: *14*

School: *Methodist College, Belfast*

Favourite subject: *PE/Games*

Special interests: *ice-skating and bowling*

Favourite food: ***challah** (plaited Jewish bread), Indian and Chinese food, and pizza*

Favourite Jewish festival: *New Year (**Rosh Hashanah**) and **Tu B'Shevat** (tree-planting festival)*

My views on Judaism: *"I'm a non-Orthodox, liberal Jew. I only attend the synagogue on special occasions but enjoy Sabbath as a fun day when I don't have to do any work. I see my religion as very personal, involving prayer and deep thinking."*

Activity

Discovering differences

Both Zoe and Adam enjoy going to school but they find that their religion marks them out as different. Here's what they say:

Adam: *"I'm the only Jew in our school and my friends don't know anything about what being a Jew is all about."*

Zoe: *"My friends accept me for who I am, but they know very little about my faith."*

If you had a Jewish friend what questions would you ask them about their faith? Can you think of ways of finding answers to your questions?

At home

Home life is very important in Jewish religion and culture. Many families, like Adam and Zoe's, have regular prayers and celebrations at home during the Sabbath meal as well as on special occasions.

One of the most significant Jewish festivals, **Passover (Pesach)**, is a very important home-based celebration (you can read about it on page 39).

Many Jewish families display special symbols and objects relating to their faith in their homes. Outside most Jewish homes there is a **mezuzah** (see below) at the front door, and inside there may be a **menorah**, a **star of David** and a picture of the Western Wall.

Star of David

Menorah

A mezuzah is a decorated container that is fixed to a doorpost. Inside is a very small scroll. Written on the scroll is a prayer from the Torah called the **Shema** (you can read it on page 41). Religious Jews touch the mezuzah as they enter and leave the house.

Activity

Symbols

On your own, make a note of what symbols are important to you.

What meaning do these symbols have for you?

Can you think how the meaning might be different for other people?

Jewish people are proud of their symbols but there is political conflict in Israel so these symbols sometimes annoy others. In just the same way, in Northern Ireland the display of symbols of one religious tradition may offend those of a different tradition.

Remember the importance of religious symbols for believers. Discuss in groups how it might be possible to display these symbols without annoying others.

Food

Jews have laws which say what foods should and shouldn't be eaten, how to prepare food properly, and what foods shouldn't be eaten together. Food which is considered proper for eating is called **kosher**.

Not all Jews apply the food laws in the same way. Zoe and her family are careful not to eat pork, but apart from that they are not strict about observing the food laws. It is difficult to find kosher food or kosher restaurants in Northern Ireland.

Adam's family eat only kosher foods and his mum has had a major influence in bringing these foods to Northern Ireland.

Kosher food

Word Bank

Challah: special plaited bread served on the Sabbath

Chanukah: the winter Festival of Lights (see page 39). The 'ch' is pronounced as the 'gh' in 'lough'.

Herbivores: animals which do not eat meat

Kosher: food that is fit to be eaten, according to Jewish dietary laws

Menorah: a seven-branched candlestick – a very old symbol of Judaism

Mezuzah: a small box containing words from the Torah (the Shema) usually placed on the doorpost of Jewish houses

Pesach: Hebrew for Passover – a festival which celebrates the Jews' escape from slavery in Egypt (you can read about this in Exodus 12)

Rosh Hashanah: a festival which marks the Jewish New Year

Shema: literally 'hear' – a Jewish statement of faith based on passages from the Torah

Star of David: a six-pointed star which symbolises Judaism. This is now one of the most familiar Jewish symbols, and is also found on the flag of Israel.

Tu B'Shevat: Jewish festival of new year for trees – a time of thanksgiving and tree-planting

Yom Kippur: the Day of Atonement – a Jewish holiday and day of fasting

Dietary laws (laws about food)

Jewish dietary laws involve preparing food carefully according to Biblical principles.

The only animals which can be eaten (kosher) are those which chew the cud *and* have cloven hooves, such as cattle and sheep.

All kosher animals are also **herbivores**.

Chickens, ducks, turkeys and geese are also allowed, but not birds of prey. These animals are specially slaughtered by kosher butchers.

Milk and meat must be kept separately and not cooked or served together, and utensils used for these must be washed and stored separately.

Who are we?

The Belfast Synagogue

Northern Ireland's only synagogue was built in 1964 and is on the Somerton Road in North Belfast.

It hosts religious services, annual festivals, and various educational and social activities for its members.

There are now only about 200 active members of the synagogue, based almost all in Belfast, although there are others with a Jewish family background living in Northern Ireland.

A Jewish rabbi

A rabbi is the person who leads the worship in a Jewish synagogue.

For many years the Jewish community in Belfast didn't have a rabbi but in 2002 Rabbi Citron and his family arrived to take up the position.

Rabbi Citron and family

The Jewish community in Belfast is proud of its history and the contribution its members have made locally and internationally. One man who is still remembered is **Otto Jaffe**.

Otto Jaffe

Otto Jaffe was Lord Mayor of Belfast twice. He was born in 1846 in Hamburg, Germany. As a child, he was taken to Belfast where his father had set up a linen business.

After working in New York for a while, Otto took over the family firm, which became the largest linen exporter to Europe.

Otto was Lord Mayor of Belfast in 1899 and 1904 and High Sheriff in 1901. He became Sir Otto and headed the Jewish community. He gave many gifts to the city.

Otto and his family felt unwelcome in Belfast after the start of World War I, not because they were Jews but because they were German.

They left to live in England where he died in 1929.

Activity

Prejudice

How do you think the Jaffe family felt when they had to leave their home in Belfast?

Do you know of other situations where people have had to leave their homes because of **racism**, **anti-Semitism** or other sorts of **prejudice**?

Imagine you were living in Belfast at the time the Jaffe family were leaving for London. Write a letter to a newspaper expressing your concern and saying how sorry you are that they had to leave.

Weekly activities in the synagogue

Even though the Belfast Jewish community is small, the synagogue is busy most weeks, serving as a community centre. The building with its various rooms is open each day for members to use.

There are many guided tours of the synagogue for schools, church groups and community groups. There is also a weekly Pensioners' Club, the **Cheder** for children, and a monthly kosher food delivery.

Morning prayers In the synagogue

At least twice a week members meet in the synagogue for morning prayers. For morning prayers and for Sabbath services to take place there must be at least ten men present.

Cheder

Cheder (the 'ch' is pronounced as the 'gh' in 'lough') is a school for Jewish children up to the age of 12. They have fun together and learn about their religion.

Cheder is held in the Belfast Synagogue every Sunday morning during school terms. Read the extract from the Cheder Newsletter on the opposite page to find out what children do there.

Cheder performance for Chanukah

Preparing for Chanukah at Cheder

Cheder Newsletter

Belfast Cheder   Volume No 1
Issue No 1   Sun 9 Nov 2003

News from the classroom

Walk into one of the two classrooms of our growing Cheder and you're bound to find a lively bunch of kids happily engaged in their learning.

Class 1

Some of our newer (and younger) faces at Cheder can now greet each other in Hebrew – "Shalom"… They are also busy learning lots of new songs …

Class 2

There is so much to learn about each Jewish holiday! This year this class will cover just as many of those details as possible … After mastering the art of blowing the shofar they learned about the importance of repentance. The story of Yonah illustrates that point as well …

Activity

Finding out

The children attending the Cheder class were spending time finding out about their own religion.

What connections do you have with religion and what do you know about your own tradition? If you are not religious, do you have any strong beliefs or opinions and what influences you in these?

In either case, take some time to find out about your own religious or non-religious outlook on life. Then make a presentation to your class about your religion or the influences which shape your opinions on the big questions in life such as life and death, and right and wrong.

Word Bank

Anti-Semitism: prejudice and discrimination against Jewish people

Cheder: children's meeting for learning about the Jewish faith

Shalom: means 'peace' – a Jewish greeting or farewell

Shofar: a ram's horn which is blown like a trumpet in the synagogue on Rosh Hashanah. Its sound represents a call to repentance.

Yonah: Jonah – a Jewish prophet

The Holocaust

The **Holocaust** is the name given to the terrible **persecution** of Jews, gypsies, homosexuals and others in Europe under the **Nazis** during **World War II**.

When Hitler came to power in Germany in 1933 Jews had all their rights taken away. They were banned from doing everyday things such as going to the park or theatre. Before long Jewish people and businesses were attacked.

When World War II began, large numbers of Jews were taken to **death camps** where many were murdered and others died because of the terrible conditions. Jews call this time of persecution the **'Shoah'**, which means 'calamity'.

Helen Lewis is a Holocaust survivor who now lives in Belfast. In a book about her experience she describes what it felt like to be a Jew in Czechoslovakia in the early 1940s:

"By 1941 the daily onslaught of vicious anti-Semitism from the newspapers and radio had prepared the ground for a new anti-Jewish law that made all previous ones look like harmless games: the introduction of the yellow star, to be worn in public at all times by all Jews over the age of six ... In the streets of Prague we became painfully aware of the stares of passers-by, some embarrassed, some openly hostile, some even surprised if one did not seem to look Jewish ... Some people did not leave their homes any longer; others tried to be philosophical; a few committed suicide."

Helen Lewis, *A Time to Speak* (Blackstaff Press, 1992)

Activity

Research

Find out more about how Jewish people under Nazi rule were treated at this time.

The Farm

Just before the start of World War II, the Nazis allowed some Jewish children to leave Germany, but their parents couldn't come with them. Many children were sent to safety in other countries, including Britain and Ireland.

Some came to Northern Ireland where they lived in a farm near Millisle, on the coast of the Ards Peninsula. After the war some of the children stayed on and settled in Northern Ireland.

Memorial plaque at the Belfast Synagogue

Activity

A virtual visit

There are major Holocaust museums in London, Washington and Israel. Look at the following web sites to go on a virtual visit:

Yad Vashem Museum, Israel
(www.yadvashem.org)

United States Holocaust Memorial Museum
(www.ushmm.org)

If you are in London, you might also visit the Holocaust Exhibition at the Imperial War Museum.

"Since Abraham the first Jew, nearly four millennia ago, Judaism and the Jewish people have learned to survive and sometimes in truly terrible conditions."
Rabbi Citron

Holocaust Memorial Day

Holocaust Memorial Day is held on 27 January to mark the liberation of **Auschwitz**, a Nazi death camp in Poland. The event was first officially marked in the UK in 2000 and in Northern Ireland in 2002.

In 2004 the main UK Holocaust Memorial Day event took place in Belfast when people of all faiths gathered at the Waterfront Hall to remember victims of the Holocaust. You can find out more at www.holocaustmemorialday.gov.uk.

The Holocaust is sometimes called an act of **genocide**. This means it was an attempt to wipe out a whole race of people. Sadly, there have been other times since the Holocaust when genocide has taken place, for example in Bosnia during the 1990s and in Rwanda in 1994.

Prince Edward, along with the Head of the Northern Ireland Civil Service and the Lord Mayor of Belfast, signing the Book of Commitment at the Waterfront Hall in January 2004

Holocaust memorial plaque at the Belfast Synagogue

Activity

Planning a memorial event

The Holocaust took place many years ago. As a class, think about why people choose to remember it still.

Imagine your class was asked to organise an event in your school for Holocaust Memorial Day.

What kind of things might you include in the programme?

What speakers might you invite?

Use your answers to these questions to design a possible programme.

Learning from the past

Find out some more details about examples of genocide such as those in Bosnia, Rwanda or Cambodia.

Discuss what lessons you think we should learn from cases of genocide and mass-killing which have happened in the past.

Can you suggest ways in which such terrible events could be stopped from happening again?

Use the ideas from your discussion to write a letter to a politician or world leader to tell them what you feel about current conflicts. Suggest some peaceful solutions.

Word Bank

Death camp: also known as concentration camp – a place where Jews were sent by the Nazis to be brutally treated and murdered

Genocide: the deliberate wiping-out of a particular nationality or ethnic group

Holocaust: the mass murder of Jews, gypsies, homosexuals and others by the Nazis during World War II

Shoah: Hebrew word which means 'calamity' and refers to the mass murder of Jews during World War II

How do we worship?

Jewish people should pray three times a day – morning, afternoon and evening. There are extra prayers on Sabbaths and festivals. Many of these prayers take place in the home but Jews also gather for prayer in the synagogue.

The synagogue

In the Talmud the synagogue is described as a 'little sanctuary'. The Romans destroyed the Temple in Jerusalem in 70 CE. Since then, Jewish worship has been completely centred around the home and the synagogue.

The central feature of a synagogue is the **Holy Ark (Aron Hakodesh)** which is set into the wall that faces Jerusalem. During services the congregation faces the Ark, and so they are facing Jerusalem too.

Inside the Ark are the scrolls of the Torah. They are taken out for readings during services, and sometimes they are all carried around the synagogue.

Above the Ark a light burns – the **Ner Tamid** (everlasting light) – to symbolise the eternal presence of God with his people.

Facing the Ark, on a central raised platform, there is a reading desk. The Torah is chanted and sermons are preached from here, showing that the Law is higher than humankind.

In front of the Ark there is usually a seven-branched candlestick – the menorah. Above the Ark you can see the Hebrew words (or initial letters) of

Torah scrolls in the Holy Ark

the Ten Commandments (see the picture on page 44). It is also quite common to find the words "Know before whom you stand" written in Hebrew near or at the Ark. Another symbol now often found in synagogues is the Star of David.

In Orthodox synagogues men and women are normally separate. Women and children sit in a gallery, or even behind a screen.

The Belfast synagogue is quite modern in style and shape, and the beams of the ceiling make the shape of the Star of David.

The Holy Ark inside the Belfast Synagogue

Interior of the Belfast Synagogue – you can see the reading desk in the centre and the star-shaped beams of the ceiling.

Sabbath

The Jewish Sabbath is from Friday night to Saturday night. It is a reminder that God rested on the seventh day after creating the world. It is a day of family celebration and prayers, and the Friday evening Sabbath meal is really important.

A personal view of the Sabbath by Zoe Angel:

"I observe the Sabbath as a fun time when I don't do any work, and I might go shopping or spend time relaxing.

I usually only attend the synagogue in Belfast on special occasions because it's difficult to understand what is going on when you don't understand Hebrew. Instead I try to worship in my own way.

Three or four times a year I also attend Sabbath services at the Reformed Synagogue in Manchester which I really enjoy."

A Sabbath meal in the Angel household

Zoe Angel and her family celebrate the Sabbath meal together on Friday nights. Often friends or other family members join them for this special occasion. She helps to set the table and prepare the candles which are lit during the meal.

Zoe's mum is Jewish and her dad is Christian, so her mum leads the Sabbath worship in their house.

The meal begins with Zoe's mum, Sarah, making a blessing over the wine (and non-alcoholic grape juice for the children) and breaking up two loaves of bread.

Everyone takes a drink before the starter is served. After the starter there is a prayer of blessing over the children and then everyone eats the main course and dessert.

Daily prayer

"Prayer is a regular part of the Jewish day. Since the destruction of the second Temple in 70 CE our homes have become our temple, a place of worship. We say the Shema as we come in and go out, on rising and going to bed. This prayer reminds us that G_d is one. On the Sabbath we say special prayers and blessings."

Zoe's mum, Sarah

Jewish man wearing a prayer shawl

Activity

Special meals

It is important in the Jewish tradition that families share a meal time around a table.

Discuss why you think that it is important for them to do this.

Do you think that it is important to eat with your family at meal times?

Decide on an occasion when you might have a family celebration. Plan a celebration meal and then prepare a letter of invitation for your guests. In your letter explain the reasons why you think it is important to meet and eat together.

Rest and leisure

Many Jewish people take the Sabbath very seriously and follow the strict behaviour of 'a day of rest'.

Some members of other religious faiths also observe a special day for worship and rest.

Make two lists on a piece of paper. In one list, put reasons for having a day of rest. In the other list, put reasons for *not* having a day of rest.

When you have finished, discuss how important a day of rest is for people today.

Word Bank

G_d: Orthodox Jews avoid using the holy name of God (see page 20 for more information on this), and therefore in English it is often written as: 'G_d'.

Holy Ark: the place at the front of the synagogue where the Torah scrolls are kept

Ner Tamid: the everlasting light, close to the Ark in the synagogue, representing the eternal presence of God

What is there to celebrate?

Celebrating festivals is a very important part of Judaism, and there are lots to celebrate! Some of the main Jewish festivals are **Rosh Hashanah**, **Passover** and **Chanukah**. You might like to find out more about other important festivals such as **Yom Kippur**, **Shavuot**, **Sukkot** and **Simchat Torah**.

Rosh Hashanah

Rosh Hashanah is the Jewish New Year. It is held in autumn and is the anniversary of creation. In the year 2000 of the Christian era the world was 5,760 years old according to Jewish tradition.

The 10 days from Rosh Hashanah to Yom Kippur, the Day of Atonement, are days of fasting and **penitence**.

Passover

The feast of Passover is held by Jews each spring to remember the escape of their ancestors from slavery in Egypt. A ritual and highly symbolic **Seder** meal is eaten. It consists of bitter herbs, lamb, apple, nuts and spices with wine, vegetables, and roasted egg.

A Seder plate

Chanukah

Chanukah is also known as the Jewish **Festival of Lights**. It is celebrated during December and lasts for eight days. Lamps are lit, prayers are recited, gifts are exchanged and Jews renew their commitment to God.

Chanukah is a festival which children particularly enjoy as it is a time for special foods such as **latkes** and doughnuts. They get a chance to take part in the celebrations in lots of different ways. The children from the Belfast Synagogue prepare a special service for adults. They dress up in Chanukah costumes and retell the story of Chanukah in their own way.

Chanukah celebrations

Rabbi and children at Chanukah

"My favourite festival is Chanukah. I like making and eating latkes and doughnuts and lighting the candles each night."

Adam Taylor

The story of Chanukah

In the second century BCE, Greeks ruled over the land of Palestine. They treated the Jews who lived there badly and changed the Jewish Temple in Jerusalem into a place to worship the Greek gods.

One man, **Judah**, was determined to reclaim the Temple for the Jews. He and his brothers formed an army to fight the Greeks. They called themselves the '**Maccabees**' which means 'hammers'.

After three years of fighting they defeated the Greeks and reclaimed the Temple. They had to remove all the symbols of the Greek gods and replace them with Jewish symbols.

Every Jewish place of worship also has a special lamp called a Ner Tamid which is always kept alight to remind worshippers of the presence of God. When Judah and his brothers came to light the lamp they realised that they had only enough oil to last one day. Miraculously, the lamp stayed alight for eight days.

To remind Jews of this miracle and the belief that God is with them in times of trouble, Jews light candles on an eight-branched candlestick during the Chanukah festival.

This banner shows another way to spell Chanukah.

Activity

Celebrations

In pairs, make a note of important events from the past which Jews celebrate and remember.

Why do you think it is important to celebrate or remember events from the past?

Think of important events or times in your own life. Make a timeline and place the events on the line with a small symbol or drawing to illustrate each event.

Decide which were happy occasions that you might celebrate and which were important moments that should be remembered, even though they may not have been particularly happy (you could illustrate this difference on your timeline too).

Now consider how you might mark each event in the future, if you had the chance. Again add a symbol or picture to your timeline to show this.

You could use your timeline as inspiration for a poem, drawing or painting called 'This Life'.

Word Bank

Latkes: potato pancakes

Penitence: being sorry for your sins and asking for forgiveness

Seder: the special symbolic meal eaten in the home during the festival of Passover

What gives life meaning?

For Jews, the meaning of life could be said to be found in relationships. They have a relationship with God and also with each other.

Beliefs about God

Jews believe their relationship with God is personal. It is based on an agreement made between God and Abraham. This agreement is called the covenant. You can read about it in Genesis 17.

God promised to make Abraham the father of many nations, and every generation would have a special link with God. In return, all Abraham's male descendants were to be circumcised, as a symbol of this covenant.

The birth of boys is still marked by **circumcision** today. This is when the foreskin of a boy's penis is removed.

The ceremony is carried out by a person who is trained for the job and is done either at home or in the synagogue.

The birth of girls in Jewish communities is celebrated by a naming ceremony at the local synagogue. The girl's father blesses the reading of the Torah and prayers are said for the mother and child.

At the time of Abraham, many people believed that there were a lot of gods, but Abraham believed that there was only one God.

The belief in one God is still central to Judaism and each morning and evening Jews recite the Shema (from the Hebrew word for 'hear'). It is a simple statement of faith from the Bible (Deuteronomy 6:4–5). Read it below.

Beliefs about tradition

Being Jewish is not just about what you think or believe. It is about what you do as well. Traditions such as festivals, times of prayer and other rituals help to give life meaning. When they do them Jews feel part of an ancient faith and culture. One such tradition is **Bar** or **Bat Mitzvah**.

Bar or Bat Mitzvah

Jews say that a boy has become an adult when he is 13 years old. On this day, he becomes Bar Mitzvah ('son of the commandment'). On the first Sabbath after his thirteenth birthday there is a special ceremony. He is called forward to read in Hebrew from the Torah and the Prophets, and receives his father's blessing.

Adam Taylor dressed for his Bar Mitzvah, wearing the tallit and tefillin

After the ceremony at the synagogue there is a meal arranged by the parents. During this, the boy gives a mini-sermon in which he thanks his parents and guests for their gifts.

Once he has become Bar Mitzvah he is a man in the eyes of the community and may now wear a **tallit** and the **tefillin** (look these up in the Wordbank!). He may also be called upon for the great privilege of reading from the Torah at a synagogue service.

The Shema
Hear, O Israel!
The Lord is our God, the Lord is one!
And you shall love the Lord your God
     with all your heart
     and with all your soul
     and with all your might.

In some communities, girls may mark becoming an adult at the age of 12. Their ceremony is called a Bat Mitzvah ('daughter of the commandment') ceremony. This is meant to encourage girls to have a more active role.

The Bat Mitzvah is similar to the Bar Mitzvah, but in Orthodox synagogues girls would not be called to read from the Torah. Instead, they do a project on some aspect of Judaism and present it after Sabbath service or on some other occasion.

One of the young people from the Belfast Synagogue has described his own Bar Mitzvah:

"One of the milestones for a boy in the Jewish religion is to achieve his Bar Mitzvah. This is acknowledged by reading from the Torah, on the day of his thirteenth birthday. I accomplished my Bar Mitzvah with great satisfaction and made my parents proud, as I had to study very hard for a long time prior to this."

Beliefs about family and community

An enormous part of what it means to be Jewish is being part of a family and wider Jewish community.

Even many Jews who do not have a strong religious faith still feel Jewish by enjoying Jewish food, music and culture.

Activity

Becoming an adult

In groups discuss:

- At what age do you think children become adults?
- What are the main differences between being a child and being an adult? (You might consider different rights and responsibilities.)
- In your opinion, when is a child ready to become an adult?

You could use the ideas from your discussion to give your opinions in a piece of writing called 'Coming of Age'.

Word Bank

Bar Mitzvah: meaning 'son of the commandment'. A Jewish boy reaches adulthood on his thirteenth birthday, when a special ceremony is held. Bar Mitzvah can refer to the boy himself or to the ceremony.

Bat Mitzvah: meaning 'daughter of the commandment'. It can refer to the girl herself or the ceremony.

Tallit: a prayer shawl

Tefillin: small boxes containing the words of the Shema. They are bound around the arm and forehead so as to be close to the heart and mind. They are sometimes called phylacteries.

How do I know what's right and wrong?

When deciding what is right or wrong, Jews look for guidance from God through the Torah, other parts of the Hebrew Bible and also the Talmud.

Although these were written long ago, Jews believe that they still have meaning today because they set down moral values that never change – such as the belief that humans are made in God's image.

Jews believe that the Ten Commandments are important moral guidelines for all people. The commandments are what all of the Law is based on, but Jews also have 603 more commandments – 357 of these are negative and 246 are positive.

Like everyone else, different Jewish people have different views on how important their rules and traditions are. Some keep them quite strictly, but others are not so strict. You have already read different views by Adam and Zoe on dietary laws (page 29). Other issues on which Jews have different opinions include:

- the role of women
- keeping the Sabbath
- marriage and sexuality
- war and peace

Jewish scriptures

The first five books of the Hebrew Bible are

- Genesis
- Exodus
- Leviticus
- Numbers
- Deuteronomy

These books are known as the Torah. They were revealed to Moses by God.

The Ten Commandments, found in the book of Exodus, are the main rules by which Jews live their lives.

Other books which, along with the Torah, make up the Jewish scriptures are gathered into collections known as the **Prophets** and the **Writings**.

Jews also study other traditional teachings, collected over many centuries, known as the Talmud.

A scroll of the Book of Esther. The Torah is also kept on scrolls like this.

The following story is one of many used by the rabbis to say how important good relationships in the home are.

"Rabbi, what shall I do?" the man asked. "My son is drifting into evil ways."

"You must love him," replied the rabbi.

"But he lies, cheats and works on the Sabbath!"

"Oh, that's different," said the rabbi. "In that case you must love him even more!"

Rosemary Rivett (ed.), *Relationships: Self, Others and God* (RE Today Services, 2004)

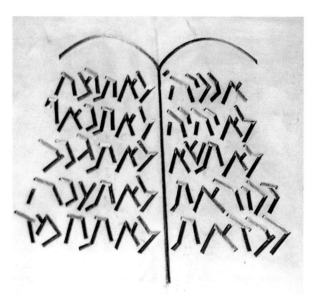

The Hebrew inscription above the Ark in the Belfast Synagogue, which represents the Ten Commandments

Activity

Rules and traditions

Many Jews believe that the Ten Commandments are a basis for a good way of life for all people. Do you agree? Why, or why not?

All religions emphasise the importance of moral behaviour. In groups, talk about what you think are the ten most important rules for people in the twenty-first century. Present your findings to the class and explain why you have chosen each rule.

What traditions are important to you? Write them down and share your thoughts with others in the class, or in your group.

Should traditional values be upheld at all costs?

The Ten Commandments

"I am the Lord your God who brought you out of Egypt, where you were slaves. Worship no god but me.

Do not make for yourselves images ... Do not bow down to any idol or worship it ...

Do not use my name for evil purposes ...

Observe the Sabbath and keep it holy ...

Respect your father and your mother ...

Do not commit murder.

Do not commit adultery.

Do not steal.

Do not accuse anyone falsely.

Do not desire another man's house ... or anything else that he owns."

Exodus 20:2–17

Word Bank

Prophets: the historical and prophetic books in the Hebrew Bible (Joshua, Judges, 1 and 2 Samuel, 1 and 2 Kings, Isaiah, Jeremiah, Ezekiel, Hosea, Joel, Amos, Obadiah, Jonah, Micah, Nahum, Habakkuk, Zephaniah, Haggai, Zechariah and Malachi)

Writings: the other books of the Hebrew Bible, not in the Torah or the Prophets (Ruth, Job, Psalms, Proverbs, Ecclesiastes, Song of Songs, Lamentations, Esther, Daniel, Ezra, Nehemiah, and 1 and 2 Chronicles)

Learning about and learning from Judaism

As a result of working on this unit on Judaism you should know about:

• Judaism as a world religion
• the Jewish community in Northern Ireland
• how some Jews worship
• important Jewish festivals
• key Jewish beliefs
• some Jewish teaching about right and wrong

You should also have had an opportunity to reflect on the following themes from your own point of view:

• dealing with difference
• symbols
• prejudice
• remembrance
• special meals
• rest and leisure
• celebrations
• coming of age
• rules and traditions

And you should have developed skills in:

• discussion
• thinking
• ICT
• working with others
• making presentations

Activity

Themes

Look at the themes in the list on the left and discuss in class what you have learnt from the Jewish religion.

Choose one of the themes and write an essay, a poem, or a letter about your own thoughts on it.

Activity

Evaluation

Now try to complete these statements honestly:

One thing I did very well during this unit was…

The reason I did well was…

One thing I could have done better was…

The reason I didn't do so well was…

Ways in which I want to improve my work in the future are…

Hinduism

What is Hinduism?

Hinduism is the world's oldest living religion.

Hinduism started in India about 3,500 years ago, although it is thought that some of its religious traditions may go back about 5,000 years. Unlike most other religions, there was no single founder of the Hindu traditions.

There are about 900 million Hindus worldwide. It is the most popular religion in India.

Varieties of Hinduism

It is important to understand that Hinduism is a religion of great variety, There are many **sects** which have all developed in different ways but which share the same scriptures and sacred texts. It may be better to speak of 'Hinduisms' rather than one single religious tradition.

For Hindus it is not so important which path you follow, so long as you do follow a spiritual path.

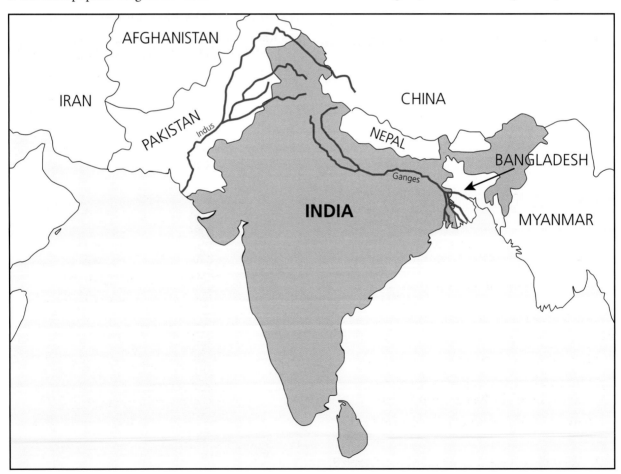

'Hinduism' is really a term used by travellers to India in the eighteenth and nineteenth centuries (1700s and 1800s) to describe the different but connected religious ideas, cultures and philosophies which they found there.

The word 'Hindu' comes from the **Sanskrit** term to describe India – **Sapta Sindhu** (pronounced Hapta Hindu) – the land of seven great rivers.

Sindhu is also the name of the **River Indus**, which is in Pakistan. Invading Greeks under Alexander the Great dropped the letter 'H', so it became Indus. This is where the word 'India' comes from.

Hindus often refer to their faith as **Sanatana Dharma**, which means eternal law or order.

The **Hare Krishna** movement is one of the best known of the many different forms of Hinduism. It has many converts from Western countries. A famous convert was the guitarist from the Beatles pop group, George Harrison (1943–2001).

Beliefs

Hindus believe in one **Supreme Being – Brahman** – that contains every characteristic of the universe and is both male and female, beautiful and ugly, creative and destructive.

However, Hindus think that it is impossible for humans to understand this Supreme Being. It is easier to think of God as a person, like a father or a mother, or as a symbol, such as fire or water. It is up to each individual to decide how they imagine God.

Hindus represent some of these different ways of thinking about God as **avatars** (gods). There are thousands of avatars but the most important of these are:

- **Brahma** (the creator god)
- **Vishnu** (the preserver god, who appeared on earth as **Lord Krishna** or **Lord Rama**)
- **Shiva** (god of destruction; also the Lord of the Dance).

Together these three gods are called the **Trimurti**.

Hindus believe in **reincarnation**. This is the cycle of birth, death and rebirth. When a person dies, the **soul** moves on to another being, which may be a person or an animal.

They hope to escape from this cycle of rebirth to achieve union with Brahman. This can be achieved by spiritual knowledge, gained through **meditation**, or by good deeds or devotion.

The actions which affect rebirth are known as **karma**.

A good karma in this life will mean a good life next time.

A bad karma in this life will mean a hard life next time.

Hindu scriptures

There are many sacred books in Hinduism. They are written in the ancient Indian language of Sanskrit.

The oldest of these are the **Vedas** which include the **Rig Veda** (the earliest) and the **Upanishads**, which means 'lessons' or 'wise teachings'.

Other sources of sacred writings are the **Mahabharata** and the **Ramayana**. These contain many stories about Hindu gods and goddesses.

One of the best known of these stories is the **Bhagavad Gita** – the Song of God – which outlines how all living beings are eternal and spiritual by nature. The Bhagavad Gita also teaches how to develop love for God and the creation.

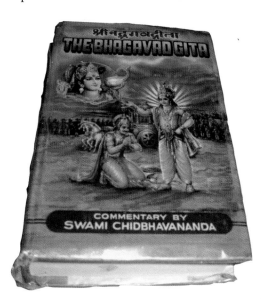

Brahman, Brahma and Brahmin

It is easy to become confused by these three names. They have different meanings.

- **Brahman**: the Supreme Being – ultimate reality
- **Brahma**: the creator god
- **Brahmin**: a priest, or the Hindu social grouping a priest belongs to

The most familiar sign or symbol of Hinduism is the lettering for the word **OM** (sometimes 'Aum') in the ancient language of Sanskrit.

No one is certain of the origins of the symbol but Hindus believe the sound symbolises the entire universe.

Hindus use the sound to help them meditate.

Gandhi

Probably the most famous Hindu of the twentieth century (1900s) was Mohandas K Gandhi.

Time Life Pictures / Getty Images

He trained in England as a lawyer. Then he became a social and political reformer who campaigned for the independence of India at a time when it was ruled by Britain.

Although he wanted the British to leave India, he strongly believed that it should not be done through fighting. He encouraged Indians to use non-violent ways to make their opinions known.

While he was a committed Hindu, Gandhi was also very influenced by Christianity and believed in the ultimate unity of all the world's religions.

He was particularly upset at the conflict between Hindus and Muslims and worked hard to help them get along better.

He was assassinated (killed) in 1948 by a member of an extremist Hindu nationalist movement.

Hinduism in Northern Ireland

According to the 2001 census, there are about 1,000 Hindus living in Northern Ireland. The Hindu community themselves think there are more like 2,000. Most of them live in the Greater Belfast area, parts of mid-Ulster and Londonderry. Many of these families came originally from the same area of North-West India.

In Belfast there is a flourishing **Indian Community Centre**, and there is a Hare Krishna temple in Dunmurry. Both communities work closely together.

The Hindu temples in Northern Ireland host religious services, marriages and a great number of festivals throughout the year.

Hare Krishna Temple in Dunmurry

Indian Community Centre in Belfast

Word Bank

Avatar: an incarnation of a god (for example, Krishna is an avatar of Vishnu)

Bhagavad Gita: an important Hindu scripture

Brahma: the Hindu creator god

Brahman: the Supreme Being

Brahmin: a priest, or the Hindu social grouping a priest belongs to

Karma: the actions that affect a person's future life

Mahabharata and Ramayana: ancient epics containing stories about the Hindu gods

Om/Aum: the Sanskrit lettering for this word is the most familiar symbol of Hinduism.

Reincarnation: the cycle of birth, death and rebirth

Rig Veda: the earliest of the Hindu scriptures or Vedas

Sanskrit: the ancient Indian language of the Hindu scriptures

Shiva: the Hindu god of destruction

Trimurti: refers collectively to Brahma, Vishnu and Shiva

Upanishads: Hindu writings which explain the Vedas' teachings

Vedas: the earliest of the Hindu scriptures

Vishnu: the Hindu preserver god

Activity

WebQuest

Explore this religion further by trying the WebQuest at www.colourpoint.co.uk/extra/localglobal

Who am I?

Let's find out about two young people from the Hindu community in Northern Ireland: Vishal and Laxshmi.

Profile

Name: *Vishal Sridhar*

Age: *12*

School: *Belfast Royal Academy*

Favourite subject: *Chemistry*

Special interests: *cricket, football, reading, badminton, writing stories*

Favourite music: *rock and **bhangra***

Favourite food: ***mater panneer***

Favourite festival: ***Diwali***

The best thing about being a Hindu: *Hinduism is the oldest and most interesting religion in the world and the ancient culture is very important to me. I enjoy going to the Hindu temple to praise the gods and eat a delicious meal.*

Profile

Name: *Laxshmi Kashyap*

Age: *14*

School: *Balmoral High School*

Favourite subject: *Music*

Special interests: *dancing, going out with friends*

Favourite music: *R&B and hip hop*

Favourite food: *Indian and Chinese*

Favourite festival: *Diwali, because it is the festival of light and it's a filling experience – it's amazing.*

The best thing about being a Hindu: *Living in Northern Ireland I enjoy being different from other people. It's also good to be part of the Indian Community Centre in Belfast where Hindus can gather and share religious moments.*

Activity

Being different

Sometimes being the odd-one-out or different from everyone else can be awkward and difficult.

In pairs, think about times when being different was a difficult experience for you.

What did others do to make the situation easier or more difficult for you?

Laxshmi thinks that being different is something special to be proud of.

Can you think of reasons why she might feel this way?

How might you act towards other people who seem to be different to stop making them feel left out?

You could use the ideas from your discussion to write guidelines for your school on how to treat visitors, new pupils and those who are different from the majority.

Home

Most Hindu homes have shrines where family worship can take place every day. There is no set time for daily prayers but most Hindus try to take part in worship (**puja**) at least once a day, in the morning or evening.

A shrine contains a **murti** (an image of the family's chosen god) as well as decorations, pictures, candles, incense sticks, offerings of food and other objects used during worship.

> It is important to note that Hindus do not worship idols. They use pictures and statues to help them focus on particular aspects of God.

© Religious Education, University of Strathclyde

A puja tray usually includes:

- **A bell**: this is rung as a call to worship for the family and to let the god know that worship is about to start.
- **An incense holder:** incense is burnt to purify the air and to help focus the mind on God.
- **A pot of water:** for ritual washing/sprinkling
- **An arti lamp:** a worshipper passes his hand over the flames from the lamp and then his forehead to receive a blessing from God.
- **A spoon:** used to sprinkle the water
- **A small pot for coloured paste:** used to bless the god and mark the forehead of the worshipper
- **Food:** offerings to the gods

Mrs Janarthanan, a Hindu mother from County Antrim, is responsible for looking after the shrine in her home and it has an important place in the everyday life of the family:

"In the morning we each shower and then pray together as a family and have a meal to start the day. There is no need to go to a temple as we have a prayer room – a puja room it is called. We try to light the lamp once in the morning and once in the evening followed by a time of prayer."

Dress

Usually Hindu young people in Northern Ireland do not wear traditional Indian dress, except when they visit the temple or on special occasions. It is common for women to wear a **sari** or **salwar-kameeze** every day.

A sari is a long piece of cloth, usually decorated with bold colours, which can be worn in different styles.

The salwar-kameeze is a long, loose tunic and a pair of pyjama-like trousers gathered at the waist and ankles.

Men usually wear a shirt and trousers to work but at home they may wear a **dhoti** – a large piece of material worn as a wrap.

Word Bank

Arti lamp: lamp used during Hindu worship

Bhangra: music which is a mixture of Western pop and traditional Punjabi music

Dhoti: a traditional Indian male garment, made of a long sheet of cotton and worn around the lower part of the body

Diwali: festival of lights, also celebrated by Sikhs

Mater panneer: mild cheese cooked with green peas and spices

Murti: an image of a god in a temple or home shrine

Puja: worship in which offerings are made to a god

Salwar-kameeze: a traditional Indian female garment in the form of a long tunic and trousers

Sari: a traditional Indian female garment, usually made from one long piece of cloth

Who are we?

The main cultural and religious centre for the Hindu community in Northern Ireland is the Indian Community Centre. The community centre building at Carlisle Circus used to be a Methodist church. It was converted for use by the Indian community in 1981 (see picture above and on page 49).

The building houses a temple, conference room, kitchen, offices, and accommodation for the temple priest.

As well as the many Indian Hindu families, the community welcomes and includes several people who do not come from Indian or Hindu backgrounds.

A sculpture of the Om symbol at the Indian Community Centre

The Indian Community Centre

"Apart from organising pujas and celebrating all major Indian festivals, we have a long list of activities every month for the young and old alike. The Indian population in Ireland has been growing considerably over the years. The Indian Community Centre has been endeavouring to maintain the rich Indian tradition and culture among the Indians living here and is making every effort to establish close contact amongst them."

Indian Community Centre information brochure

The community centre plays a very important role in welcoming new members of the Indian community to Northern Ireland. It also provides support and friendship for existing members, and helps young people to learn more about their faith and culture. Laxshmi says:

"What I enjoy most about coming to the community centre is to learn more and more about my religion."

A community prayer – **Hawan** – usually takes place once a month and is hosted by different families each month. It includes a ceremony where grains are sprinkled onto a fire. It is followed by a time of prayer in the temple and a meal in the community centre. Nisha Tandon and Sharada Bhat, development workers in Indian Community Centre, describe the Hawan ceremony and its significance:

"The holy fire (Agni the fire goddess) is lit in a special cast-iron pot called Hawan Kund. Offerings of rice, water, ghee and sweets are poured slowly and gradually into the holy fire and sacred hymns are recited. The whole ceremony lasts for about 45 minutes and then other prayers take place in the temple. After this is finished the hosts offer everyone food."

Nisha

"We pray to God to receive offerings through fire because fire is part of God. We consider God is in everything and through the fire we bring offerings to Him."

Sharada

Activity

Outside-in

Here is Mr Janarthanan describing how he and his family felt about coming to live in Northern Ireland:

"In 1990 when we arrived as a family, I was very impressed with the education system. People were very friendly.

Even though the peace process had not started at that time, the Troubles had reduced and the developments had started, so it was better.

After that we were very busy at work. The first time I started working with people, I had interaction with workers from all levels. We could see the full spectrum of the population.

After about three or four months we met a family from Indonesia who used to go to the temple often. They invited us and there we met people we have become friends with."

In pairs or in groups, imagine you were coming to Northern Ireland for the first time. What do you think you might notice that was good or bad about it?

How do you think you might make friends or get to know new people?

What might you miss about the place you were coming from?

How could the local people make your introduction to the country easier?

Use some of the ideas from your discussion to write a welcome page for people coming to live in Northern Ireland for the first time.

Activity

A common thread

At the start of a Hawan ceremony, holy thread is tied around each person's wrist. These threads symbolise being connected to one another and to God.

In what way do you feel connected to others:

• in your class?

• in your school?

• in your place of worship?

• in the wider world?

Think of some symbols which might illustrate the connection you feel with others in one of these situations. Try to draw or paint a picture to represent your thoughts.

Celebrating Hawan at the Indian Community Centre

Word Bank

Hawan: an act of worship in which grains of rice or ghee (butter used in Indian cookery) are thrown into fire

How do we worship?

"To those who are constantly devoted and worship Me with love, I give the understanding by which they can come to Me."

The Mahabharata

Worship in Hinduism is mostly personal and carried out at shrines in the home (see page 51), but temples are also an important place for Hindus to come together for worship. A temple is where **consecrated** murtis (images of gods) live and the priests who work there look after them as if they were human.

Puja, or the act of worship, is the way in which Hindus express their devotion to their god. It earns them merit for their behaviour and may help them to achieve a better rebirth.

The Hindu gods

Most Hindus believe in one God called Brahman – a Supreme Being who is beyond understanding and description. The many other gods worshipped by Hindus are thought of as different aspects of this one supreme power.

The most important of these are Brahma, Vishnu and Shiva – the Trimurti (see page 47). Also well-known are:

- **Lakshmi** (Vishnu's wife)
- **Ganesha** (the elephant-headed god)
- **Hanuman** (the monkey god).

For many Hindus, Krishna is the most popular of these manifestations of God. His name means 'the most attractive person'.

Lakshmi

Hanuman

Hindus also believe that God is present in everything that has been created. So certain rivers, lakes, trees, animals, birds and flowers are considered especially sacred. The cow, for example, is sacred in Hinduism because of its usefulness to humans.

Hindus often choose a particular god or goddess to worship as their personal god, but this does not mean that they can't worship other gods or goddesses.

It does not matter which god or gods you worship because Hindus believe:

"All gods lead to God as all rivers lead to the sea".

Bhagavad Gita

Worship at a shrine

As a sign of respect, worshippers remove their shoes before entering a Hindu temple.

Puja in a Hindu temple usually begins with the washing of the images of the gods before they are anointed with coloured marks.

Worship also involves songs, prayers, offerings of flowers and food and recitations of sacred verses.

It usually ends with the offering of the sacred flame to the gods. This is done by lighting an arti lamp. Food, which had been blessed and given as offerings to the gods, is distributed.

Arti lamp

Shrine in the Indian Community Centre

Offerings

"Puja is important to me and, being Hindu, it is my duty to do puja at least twice a day. This may include praying, lighting a candle, reading or meditation.

When doing puja I feel calm and focused. It gives me satisfaction and I enjoy taking part in it."

Raj Somasundram

Sacred rituals and ceremonies in the temple are normally led by Brahmin – priests and teachers. They are usually well-educated men who try to keep themselves pure in various ways such as eating a vegetarian diet, studying the sacred Hindu writings, avoiding alcohol, practising **yoga** and meditating.

There is one priest associated with the Indian Community Centre and he is responsible for leading worship and caring for the shrines in the temple.

Prayer and meditation

Most Hindus learn the art of meditation and prayer from a young age. Hindus believe that the material world is like an illusion because everything eventually passes away.

The only thing which will always exist is Brahman, the supreme God, but a part of Brahman also exists in all living things. This is the soul.

Meditation involves stilling the mind to purify it and focus on the soul:

"Still your mind in Me, still yourself in Me, and without a doubt you shall be united with Me, Lord of Love, dwelling in your heart".

The Mahabharata

Sharada Bhat explains:

"Meditation is a process – you start with concentrating on one thing and then you increase your connection with God. It can be a dot or a flame or any beautiful face of God – anything you feel comfortable focusing on."

Another form of meditation is yoga. This involves putting the body into various positions and using breathing techniques to discipline the mind and body so that meditation can take place.

In the UK and Ireland yoga has become a very popular method of exercise and relaxation for many people.

For most worshippers, being a Hindu is not just about attending a temple each week or month. It is a way of life. As Sharada Bhat explains:

"Practising religion and being a Hindu is part of your life and duties, which is like when you need food for your body to grow and to live; religion is to know about God and make this part of your life. It is just a way of life – it is not separate. There are always benefits when you practise the gods' way."

Activity

Using your senses

During worship, Hindus try to involve all their senses. Read the description of puja in this section and look at the puja tray on page 51. Write down how all the senses are used during worship.

Carry out a 'senses activity'. If you can, bring some things into class – things like a stone, a leaf, a shell, or a twig. Take time to use all your senses to experience each object. What does it look like? Smell like? Feel like? Can you make a noise with it?

Write down your observations.

When you have finished, think about why Hindus find it helpful to worship in the way that they do.

Word Bank

Consecrate: to make holy or sacred

Ganesha: the Hindu elephant-headed god

Hanuman: the Hindu monkey god

Lakshmi: the Hindu goddess of fortune – also Vishnu's wife

Yoga: a form of meditation achieved through mental and physical exercises

What is there to celebrate?

It is said that Hindus have a festival or celebration for every day of the year – and more besides!

Samskars

Samskars are rites of passage. That means that they are special occasions that mark important times in life such as birth, **initiation**, marriage, and death.

Shortly after birth there is a religious ceremony to welcome the child into the family. This ceremony includes putting something sweet, such as honey, on to the tongue of the baby. A prayer is made that the child's name and words may be as sweet as honey throughout life.

The Sacred Thread Ceremony

One of the most important initiation ceremonies for a boy is **Upanayana**. This is a samskar for boys between 8 and 12 years old and is often called the **Sacred Thread Ceremony**.

This ceremony is regarded as a second, spiritual birth. During the ceremony a thread of three strands is placed round the left shoulder of the boy and under his right hand. The thread represents several important Hindu beliefs and symbolises to the boy that he should have control over his thoughts, words and actions.

He recites the **Gayatri Mantra** and is given a staff which represents learning.

The ceremony is another step on a boy's spiritual path. From then on he is able to take a full part in religious ceremonies and is encouraged to study the sacred Hindu scriptures.

Gayatri Mantra

"We concentrate our minds upon the most radiant light of the Sun god, who sustains the Earth, the Interspace and the Heavens. May the Sun god activate our thoughts."

Rig Veda III.62.10

A young person's description of the Sacred Thread Ceremony

*"The ceremony began with some **mantras**. These are difficult to pronounce so the priest said them and I repeated it.*

White thread, made in India and specially designed for this ceremony, was placed on me from my shoulder to my waist. Yellow powder was then put on the thread to bless it.

For me the ceremony signified learning and spiritual knowledge. It was a commitment and a way of looking forward, of sticking to the principles of my faith. It taught me prayers which are focused, peaceful and concentrated.

This ceremony also helps to keep you organised as it teaches you to practise the prayers daily which is important!"

Raj Somasundram

Activity

A lifelong journey

Hindus believe there are four main stages to life and there are 16 different rites of passage (samskars) connected with these stages, although very few actually achieve all 16.

Imagine your own life as a journey through different stages. How would you divide it up?

What important moments would you want to mark or celebrate along the way?

Draw a diagram of your imagined journey through life. You could illustrate it too.

You could share this with friends or with your class. Point out:

- what you have done on the journey so far
- what you are most proud of
- what your aims are for the future.

Festivals

Some of the young Hindu people who belong to the Indian Community Centre have spoken of their favourite times and festivals. Diwali is a firm favourite.

> Diwali is one of the best known Hindu festivals. It is a festival of lights which marks the New Year in some parts of India.
>
> The theme is light and darkness, and Lakshmi – the goddess of fortune – is believed to visit homes that are well lit-up by lamps.
>
> There is always a special Diwali celebration at the Indian Community Centre. Many members of the community and many guests go to this. Sikhs also have their own special Diwali celebrations (see page 19).
>
> Like many Hindus, 12-year-old Poonum loves the festival of Diwali. She says:
>
> *"It's about sharing happiness."*
>
> Raj, aged 19, also loves Diwali:
>
> *"because it's all colourful and very musical. There will be dances and drama, not to mention the food!"*
>
> His sister Kousalyaa, aged 16, says:
>
> *"We get new clothes, money and jewellery."*
>
> Babu, another sixth-former, adds:
>
> *"Don't forget the fireworks!"*

Nisha Tandon and a company of dancers from the Indian Community Centre

> The spring festival of **Holi** is another well-known Hindu celebration. It is a celebration of Lord Krishna and reminds Hindus of the stories of his playfulness and practical jokes.
>
> Bonfires are lit and children throw coloured water and powders at each other.
>
> In the evening people visit friends and exchange greetings and sweets.

For the Belfast Indian community one of the biggest occasions of the year is the Belfast Mela.

Mela is an Indian summer festival and normally takes place in Belfast's Botanic Gardens towards the end of August. There are market-type stalls of many kinds, special food stalls, and a large marquee for demonstrations, workshops and performances.

It is an opportunity for the Belfast Indian community to express its identity and interests and for people from many different backgrounds to experience and enjoy Indian culture.

The Mela also includes people from other cultural traditions, such as the Chinese community. This shows the traditional Indian and Hindu attitude to **inclusion** and the celebration of **diversity**.

Enjoying the Belfast Mela

Performing at the Belfast Mela

A ctivity

Arranged marriages

Up until the nineteenth century (1800s), arranged marriages were very common in European countries, though that has now mostly changed.

In class, have a discussion about the advantages and disadvantages of arranged marriages.

Marriage

It is still very common for Hindu families to have **arranged marriages**, although some traditions are changing. Sharada Bhat compares her own marriage to that of her daughter:

"My husband and I had an arranged marriage. I did not know my future husband – I may have seen him but I did not know him. It was all organised by my parents. It was a little scary on my wedding day.

… However, it was not so simple with my daughter – her marriage was 'sort of arranged'. We found a boy through friends and family in India … and then they were introduced and they talked. It took time … and she couldn't decide.

Because she was born in a Western country, his family wondered how she would fit in. She is now living in London with her husband … and he was happy to come over and get work.

… I believe all Indian parents here would like their child to marry an Indian who has grown up with the culture."

W ord Bank

Arranged marriage: in this tradition, a person's parents choose their future husband or wife for them.

Diversity: variation and difference, especially in relation to cultures

Mela: Indian summer festival

Samskar: a Sanskrit word for the steps through life such as birth, marriage and death. Most Hindus believe there are 16 steps for higher caste Hindus.

Upanayana: an initiation ceremony for Hindu boys. It is also known as the Sacred Thread Ceremony.

A Hindu wedding

What gives life meaning?

Hindus believe that the goal of life is to be released or liberated (**moksha**) from the cycle of birth, death and rebirth and become one with Brahman.

Karma is what decides how well you have lived your life (see page 47). Every choice or action you take in this life produces either good or bad karma and, depending on the amount of each, you will receive a higher or lower position in your next life, or you may even achieve moksha.

Moksha

Moksha is liberation, but liberation from what?

Hindus believe the material world which we experience with our five senses is a kind of prison. It is not the real world. It is a distraction from what is true and eternal.

So it is necessary for a person to let go of all worldly desires and attachments. When a person is liberated from the material world, his or her soul becomes one with Brahman.

To explain this state of being, some Hindus use the image of a drop of water entering the ocean from which it came.

Activity

Life after death

In pairs discuss your ideas about life after death.

Do you think that how you choose to live your life will make a difference to what happens to you when you die?

You could carry out a survey to see how many different ideas those in your class have about life after death.

There are three main ways in which moksha can be achieved: **sannyasa**, **dharma** and **bhakti**.

Sannyasa

This is the most difficult path and involves giving up all your possessions as well as your friends and family. There are not many who choose this path to become wandering holy men or to join a **monastic** order.

Dharma

This is the way of duty and obedience. A person following this path must always try to do what is right according to their position in life (**caste** – see page 62).

Bhakti

The most common path for Hindus is bhakti. This is spiritual devotion to the gods. Worshippers must try to be aware of their god always, and regularly carry out rituals, prayer and meditation.

Whatever path a person chooses, Hindus believe they should carry it out with joy. Here are some things that members of the Indian Community Centre say about the importance of their religion to them:

"The most important thing about being a Hindu is that it is a celebration of life!"

Babu Shankar

"The main belief in Hinduism is karma; what you do today you will reap tomorrow. If you do good things to others and society, it will return to you."

Mr Janarthanan

"In Hinduism we believe God can be in any form and we can worship him through that form. Because of this there are many stories of different deities [gods] and we use these in worship and for guidance."

Sharada Bhat

Pilgrimage

Hindus often go on pilgrimages to favourite temples or holy places. The banks of the **River Ganges** are very popular for pilgrimages. Hindus believe that washing in the river is an act of devotion that can wash away bad karma.

Many Hindus from Northern Ireland make a special effort to travel to India to visit places of special importance to their family.

These trips often have religious significance as well and are connected to the celebration of certain samskars.

The River Ganges (also known as Ganga) at Varanasi

Gavin Hellier / Getty Images

How do I know what's right and wrong?

For a Hindu, every action in life is important because each action has consequences and creates either good or bad karma. So it is very important for a Hindu to consider the effect their actions or decisions will have on the people and world around them. To make the wrong choices will mean they will be punished in the next life.

Hindus are also guided in their decisions about what is right and wrong through reading their sacred writings, praying and meditating, and asking their guru or priest for advice.

Sacred writings can give direct instructions – such as the **Golden Rule**. Sometimes they provide examples of how to live through the stories of the gods. Above all, Hindus believe that life is sacred and they must try to avoid violence and killing.

Activity

My special place

Many people associate special feelings or beliefs with particular places. Sometimes the places are religious buildings but they could also be a garden, a mountain, a beach or a place they associate with a special person or time in their life.

Imagine you were asked to record a short radio slot called 'My Special Place'. Using a tape recorder or voice recorder, make a recording of your thoughts about your place. Share the results with your class.

Word Bank

Bhakti: spiritual devotion

Dharma: religious or social duty

Moksha: liberation from the cycle of rebirths

Sannyasa: renunciation (giving up)

The Golden Rule

"This is the sum of duty: do not do to others what would cause pain if done to you."

The Mahabharata

The Mahabharata is one of the most popular of the Hindu scriptures. This statement from it is sometimes called the Golden Rule. Statements like this can be found in many of the world's religions.

Activity

Making decisions

Imagine that one day your class is left without a teacher for several hours. You have been asked to complete a very important piece of work and have all promised to try your best.

One third of the class want to get all the work done to the best of their ability.

One third have no intention of keeping their promise and want to have fun while the teacher is gone.

One third aren't sure what to do; they feel worried about getting into trouble but don't really want to do the work. *[continued over page]*

In groups, discuss what you think might happen while the teacher is away.

If you had to suggest a solution to this problem what might it be?

How might the Hindu Golden Rule be helpful in this situation?

The caste system

Traditionally, Hindus have organised society in a very structured way. Each person is said to belong to a particular social group. This is often called the **caste** system. There are thousands of groups, often gathered under four main headings:

- **Brahmins** – priests

- **Kshatriyas** – soldiers

- **Vaishyas** – shopkeepers and farmers

- **Shudras** – servants

Some Hindus do not belong to any of these groups and are thought of as **Outcastes**.

For Hindus, the group a person belongs to has a very strong influence on how they live their life. They believe that it is your duty to live according to the group you are born into.

At first, the caste system was just a way of organising people to do different jobs so that society worked well and ran smoothly.

If society is thought of as a body, the Brahmins were the head, the Kshatriyas the hands, the Vaishyas the stomach, and the Shudras the legs and feet.

They were all different, but equal. Each had an important role to play to keep the body working well.

Unfortunately, through time the groups became ordered in importance and were not considered equal any more. Modern Indian governments have become very worried about how unfair the system is and have tried to ban it.

Still, many Hindus feel that belonging to a group is important. It is like being part of a large family which can offer support and help.

Animals

Hindus believe that it is important to treat other people with respect. They also believe that exactly the same applies to all living things, because every living thing has a soul.

For this reason many Hindus do not eat meat. Certain animals – such as the cow – have a special place in Hindu culture.

Activity

Animal rights

In pairs or groups, discuss whether you agree or disagree with the Hindu belief that animals should be treated with respect.

Write a speech for a debate on animal rights. In your speech, outline your opinions on caring for animals. You could consider things like:

- killing animals for food
- keeping animals in captivity
- experimenting on animals
- transporting animals.

Word Bank

Caste: the social class a person is seen to belong to

Learning about and learning from Hinduism

As a result of working on this unit on Hinduism you should know about:

- Hinduism as a world religion
- the Hindu community in Northern Ireland
- how some Hindus worship
- important Hindu gods and festivals
- key Hindu beliefs
- some Hindu teaching about right and wrong

You should also have had an opportunity to reflect on the following themes from your own point of view:

- being different
- adapting to a new environment
- connections and relationships with others
- how to use your senses
- life as a journey
- remembering your roots
- arranged marriage
- life after death
- having a special place
- making moral decisions
- animal rights

And you should have developed skills in:

- discussion
- thinking
- ICT
- working with others
- making presentations

Activity

Explore your questions

Review the work you have done on Hinduism and ask yourself if you still have any questions about this religion.

Write down the question you would most like to have answered. Perhaps your teacher could collect all the questions together and then give them out again so that you get somebody else's question.

Now to try to find some answers to the question you have been given!

You could complete this task as a homework and present your findings in the next class.

Activity

Evaluation

Now try to complete these statements honestly:

One thing I did very well during this unit was…

The reason I did well was…

One thing I could have done better was…

The reason I didn't do so well was…

Ways in which I want to improve my work in the future are…

Index